Crochet Wreath Patterns

Festive Crochet Wreath Patterns for Your Home

Copyright © 2023

All rights reserved.

DEDICATION

The author and publisher have provided this e-book to you for your personal use only. You may not make this e-book publicly available in any way. Copyright infringement is against the law. If you believe the copy of this e-book you are reading infringes on the author's copyright, please notify the publisher at: https://us.macmillan.com/piracy

Contents

Crochet and Ribbon Valentine's Wreath 1

Crochet Wreath Brooch with Bow 7

Spring Wreath 11

April Flowers Wreath 19

St. Patrick's Day Wreath 25

Tiny Crochet Wreath 30

Cream Merry Christmas Wreath 34

Cream Happy Thanksgiving 42

Cream Happy Easter Wreath 52

Crochet Wreath Patterns

Crochet and Ribbon Valentine's Wreath

Materials

With size H hook

Chain 21, SC in second chain from hook and the rest of the way down the chain, chain 1, turn (20 SC)

Rows 2-150: SC in each stitch, chain 1, turn (20 SC)

Leave a long long tail after your last row so you can stitch the edges together onto the wreath.

Crochet Wreath Patterns

When you wrap your crocheted strip around the wreath make sure your rows match up. Now take your tapestry needle and start stitch it together. It always looks like it won't work out, but keep matching up the beginning of the row to the end of the same row and it will all come together with no lumps or bumps at the end.

Crochet Wreath Patterns

With white yarn and a size G hook..

Large Snowball:

Magic Ring, chain 1 and make 5 SC in ring, continue to SC in rounds

Round 2: 2 SC in each stitch around (10 SC)

Round 3: 2 SC in first stitch, SC in next stitch, repeat around (15 SC)

Round 4: 2 SC in first stitch, SC in next two, repeat around (20 SC)

Round 5-7: SC in each stitch around (20 SC)

Round 8: SC decrease, SC in next 2, repeat around

Round 9: SC decrease, SC in next stitch, repeat around

stuff with poly-fil

Round 10: SC decrease around until closed.

Medium Snowball:

Magic Ring, chain 1 and make 5 SC in ring, continue to SC in rounds

Round 2: 2 SC in each stitch around (10 SC)

Round 3: 2 SC in first stitch, SC in next stitch, repeat around (15 SC)

Round 4-6: SC in each stitch around (15 SC)

Round 7: SC decrease, SC in next stitch, repeat around

stuff with poly-fil

Round 8: SC decrease around until closed.

Small Snowball:

Magic Ring, chain 1 and make 5 SC in ring, continue to SC in rounds

Round 2: 2 SC in each stitch around (10 SC)

Round 3-4: SC in each stitch around (10 SC)

stuff with poly-fil

Round 5: SC decrease around until closed.

Crochet Wreath Patterns

Now to make a some cute crocheted bunting!

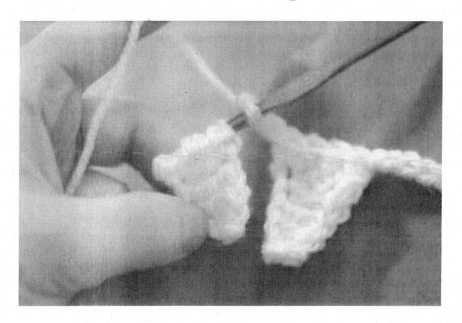

First make 4 triangle pennant flags:

Chain 6, SC in second chain from hook, HDC in next, DC in next two, TC in last. Fasten off and weave in ends.

Crochet Wreath Patterns

Now you are going to chain 10 (or so) and then single crochet into the top of the flags. Chain 3 in between the flags.

Crochet Wreath Brooch with Bow

Yarn: Red Heart Super Saver (Medium Weight Yarn) in Red, Green and White.

Hook: 4.0 mm (G) Crochet Hook

This pattern is written in U.S. Terms.

Crochet Wreath Patterns

st(s) – stitch(es)

sl st – slip stitch

ch – chain

sc – single crochet

hdc – half double crochet

dc – double crochet

tr – triple/treble crochet

tr3tog – triple/treble 3 together

Base

1. Ch-20, 1 sl st into the first stitch to make a ring.

2. Ch-4 (counts as 1 dc and one ch-1), 1 dc into the second stitch from the hook, chain 1; *1 dc, ch-1 into the next stitch*, repeat from * to * around, ch-1, sl st into the top of the initial ch-3.

3. *1 sl st into the first ch-1 space, (1 hdc, 1 dc, 1 hdc) into the next ch-1 space* repeat from * to * around. Sl st into the first hdc and finish

Crochet Wreath Patterns

off.

Bow

1. Ch-4, work 9 dc into the fourth ch from the hook, turn

2. Ch-4 (counts as 1 tr), tr3tog, ch-4 (counts as 1 tr), sl st to the next dc, sl st to the next dc.

Ch-10.

You will now be working back along the chain-10 as follows: Skip the first 3 ch sts, 1 tr in each of the next 2 sts, 1 dc in each of the next 2 sts, 1 hdc in each of the next 2 sts, 1 sc in the last st.

1 sl st to the next dc.

Ch-10.

You will now be working back along the chain-10 as follows: Skip the first 3 ch sts, 1 tr in each of the next 2 sts, 1 dc in each of the next 2 sts, 1 hdc in each of the next 2 sts, 1 sc in the last st.

1 sl st to the next dc.

Ch-4, in the next dc, tr3tog (the last tr will begin in the top of 3rd chain from the initial ch-4 of R1), ch-4 and sl st into the top of the 3rd chain.

Finish off, leaving approximately 60-cm of extra yarn to use to wrap

Crochet Wreath Patterns

around the centre portion of the bow.

This was initially designed to fit around the base of the battery operated candle – but there are many other uses for it – just by changing yarn colours, assembly and embellishments…

Crochet Wreath Patterns

Spring Wreath

Difficulty: Easy

Amount of time: Approx 8-10 hours

Materials:

For the spring wreath:

Crochet Wreath Patterns

Styrofoam wreath (any size)

Yarn color of your choice

4mm (G) hook

Yarn needle

For the crochet flowers:

Yarn in various colors

4mm (G) hook

Yarn needle

For the amigurumi bee:

Yarn in yellow, black and white

3mm (E) hook

6 mm Amigurumi eyes

Fiberfill stuffing

Yarn needle

Crochet Wreath Patterns

For the leaf garland:

Yarn in green

4mm (G) hook

Instructions:

Wreath:

Measure your Styrofoam wreath's outer circle. The area between the outer and the inner circle measured approx. 8 cm (3 inches) wide.

Now you have to crochet a piece that will fold around your wreath.

Ch 21

R1: sc in second ch from hook and in each st across (20)

Crochet Wreath Patterns

Continue until your piece is long enough to fold around your wreath.

Now, you will have to fold your piece around the wreath and using a yarn needle, sew it onto the wreath.

Flowers: Using color of your choice

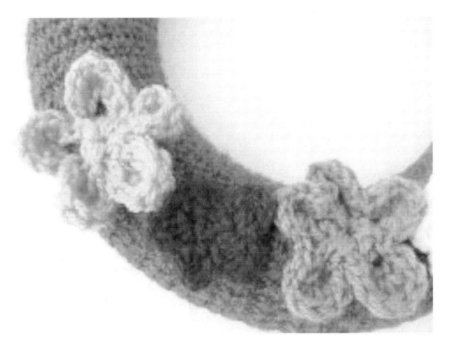

For small flower:

Ch2

Crochet Wreath Patterns

R1: 6sc in second chain from hook (6)

R2: attach new color,* ch3 (counts as first dc), 2 dc, sl st in next st, rep from* around 4 times. Fasten off.

For large flower:

Ch2

R1: 6sc in second chain from hook (6)

R2: form petals, *ch6 and sl st to center* rep from* around 4 times

R3: *ch1 and sc, hdc, 3dc, hdc, sc, sl st* rep from* around 4 times. Fasten off.

Make as many as you want.

Amigurumi Bee:

Crochet Wreath Patterns

The bee demands you know how to switch from one color to another. To change colors, crochet to the last stitch on the row. Start the last stitch by inserting the hook into the chain from the previous row and pulling a loop through. Now, with the new color, finish the single crochet by bringing a loop through the 2 stitches on the hook.

Using yellow:

Ch2

Crochet Wreath Patterns

R1: 6 sc in second ch from hook (6)

R2: 2 sc in each st around (12)

R3: 1 sc , 2 sc in next st, repeat 6 times (18)

R4: sc in each st around (18)

Change to black

R5-6: sc in each st around (18)

Change to yellow

R7: sc in each st around (18)

Change to black

R8-9: sc in each st around (18)

Change to yellow, add eyes and start to stuff

R10: 1 dec, 1 sc, repeat 6 times (12)

Change to black

R11: 6 dec, (6)

Continue to stuff

R12-13: sc in each st around (6)

Crochet Wreath Patterns

Fasten off and weave in ends.

Embroider a mouth using red thread.

Wings, make two:

Using white, Ch2

R1: 6 sc in second ch from hook (6)

R2: 1 sc, 2 sc in next st repeat two times (9)

R3-7: sc in each st around (9)

Fasten off, fold in half and sew on the bee.

Leaf garland:

Using green ch 100 and fasten off.

Crochet Wreath Patterns

April Flowers Wreath

Wreath measures 14" [35.5cm] diameter

WREATH

Wrap A around Wreath form to cover 2½" [6.5cm] completely. Glue ends to form. Wrap B around Wreath form to cover next 2½" [6.5cm].

Glue ends. Continue to wrap A and B around Wreath form, alternating colors, to cover completely.

ROUND FLOWER

Make 1 each with C, D, E and F

Ch 18.

Row 1: Sc in 2nd ch from hook, 3 sc in next 4 ch, 3 hdc in next 4 ch, 3 dc in next 4 ch, 3 tr in next 4 ch.

Fasten off, leaving a long tail for sewing.

Loosely wind into a coil with sc sts in center and sew together.

DAISY

Make 1 each with C, D, E and F Outer Petals

Ch 2.

Round 1: 8 sc in 2nd ch from hook, slip st in first sc to join – 8 sc.

Round 2: *Ch 6, sc in 2nd ch from hook, sc in next ch, hdc in next ch, dc in next 2 ch, sc in next st; repeat from * 7 more times, slip st to first

Crochet Wreath Patterns

ch – 8 petals.

Fasten off, leaving a long tail for sewing.

Inner Petals

Ch 2.

Round 1: 6 sc in 2nd ch from hook, slip st in first sc to join – 6 sc.

Round 2: *Ch 4, sc in 2nd ch from hook, hdc in next ch, dc in next ch, sc in next st; repeat from * 5 more times, slip st in first ch – 6 petals.

Fasten off, leaving a long tail for sewing.

Sew Inner Petal in center of Outer Petals.

LARGE POSY

Make 1 each with C, D, E and F

Ch 2.

Round 1: 6 sc in 2nd ch from hook, slip st in first sc – 6 sc.

Round 2: *(Ch 4, tr, ch 4, sc) in same st, *(sc, ch 4, tr, ch 4, sc) in same st; repeat from * 4 more times, slip st in first ch — 6 petals.

Fasten off, leaving a long tail.

SMALL POSY

Make 1 each with C, D, E and F

Ch 2.

Round 1: 6 sc in 2nd ch from hook, slip st in first sc.

Round 2: Ch 2, (hdc, ch 2, sc) in same st, *(sc in next st, ch 2, hdc) in same st, ch 2, sc in same st; repeat from * 4 more times, slip st in first ch — 6 petals.

Fasten off, leaving a long tail for sewing.

LEAVES

Crochet Wreath Patterns

Make 1-2 for each Flower

With G, ch 7.

Row 1: Sc in 2nd ch from hook, sc in next st, hdc in next st, dc in next st, hdc in next st, 3 sc in next st, turn to work along opposite edge of foundation ch, hdc in next ch, dc in next ch, hdc in next ch, sc in next 2 ch, slip st in first sc.

Fasten off, leaving a long tail for sewing.

FINISHING

For each Posy, sew button and small Posy to center of each Large Posy. Sew one or two leaves to back of each Posy, Daisy and Round Flower. Sew buttons to centers of Daisies and Round Flowers. Weave in ends.

Assembly

Following photo and holding flowers in place with pins, arrange flowers around front lower third of Wreath as desired, leaving one flower for hanger. When desired arrangement has been obtained, sew pieces in place.

Crochet Wreath Patterns

Hanger

With 1 strand of C and E held together, ch 80,

slip st in first ch to join. Fasten off.

Fold ch around top of wreath, pulling one folded end through opposite end for hanger.

Sew last flower in front of hanger.

Abbreviations

A, B, C = Color A, B, C; ch = chain; dc = double crochet; hdc = half double crochet; mm = millimeters; sc = single crochet; st(s) = stitch(es); tr = triple or treble crochet; [ ] = work directions in brackets the number of times specified; * or ** = repeat whatever follows the * or ** as indicated.

Crochet Wreath Patterns

St. Patrick's Day Wreath

Materials

12 in. Styrofoam wreath

7 rainbow colors worsted weight yarn (such as Lion Brand's Vanna's

Crochet Wreath Patterns

Choice in red, orange, yellow, green, blue, indigo, and violet)

black worsted weight yarn

sparkly sport weight yarn, such as Lion Brand Gold Bonbons

US G-6 / 4.0 mm crochet hook

US C-2 / 2.75 mm crochet hook

tapestry needle

hot glue gun

WREATH PATTERN

With a G hook and CA, ch 21 (or the length you need to fit around the tube of the wreath).

Row 1: 1 sc in 2nd ch from hook and each ch across, turn — 20 sts.

Row 2: Ch 1 (does not count as st here and throughout), 1 sc in each st across, drop CA turn — 20 sts.

Crochet Wreath Patterns

Row 3: Join CB, ch 1, 1 sc in each st across, turn — 20 sts.

Row 4: Ch 1, 1 sc in each st across, drop CB turn — 20 sts.

Row 5: Join CC, ch 1, 1 sc in each st across, turn — 20 sts.

Row 6: Ch 1, 1 sc in each st across, drop CC turn — 20 sts.

Row 7: Join CD, ch 1, 1 sc in each st across, turn — 20 sts.

Row 8: Ch 1, 1 sc in each st across, drop CD turn — 20 sts

Row 9: Join CE, ch 1, 1 sc in each st across, turn — 20 sts.

Row 10: Ch 1, 1 sc in each st across, drop CE turn — 20 sts.

Row 11: Join CF, ch 1, 1 sc in each st across, turn — 20 sts.

Row 12: Ch 1, 1 sc in each st across, drop CF turn — 20 sts.

Row 13: Join CG, ch 1, 1 sc in each st across, turn — 20 sts.

Repeat color sequence 8 more times for a total of 63 rows.

Fasten off, weave in ends.

GOLD COINS PATTERN

Using a C hook and the sparkly sport weight yarn, make a magic ring (as an alternative to the magic ring, you can ch 4 and join with a slip stitch in furthest chain from hook to form a ring).

Round 1: Ch 1 (does not count as st here and throughout), work 6 sc

Crochet Wreath Patterns

in ring, join — 6 sts.

Round 2: Ch 1, work 2 sc in same st as join and in each st around, join — 12 sts.

Fasten off, weave in ends.

ASSEMBLING

Use a piece of crumpled tissue paper to fill in the bottom part of the pot. Then cover the top with coins. Use a dab of hot glue to keep the coins in place. Sew or glue the pot to the center of your wreath. If desired glue a few coins around the bottom of the pot as well. You can even add a shamrock or two if you want.

Tiny Crochet Wreath

Abbreviations

US Terminology Used

Ch   Chain

Sc   Single crochet

Sl st   Slip stitch

Crochet Wreath Patterns

St/st's   Stitch/stitches

Materials

Double knit yarn (light worsted weight/#3) in green – a couple of yards

4 mm crochet hook (US 6/G UK 8)

Yarn needle

Instructions

Ch 10 (Photo 1). Join to the first st with a sl st to form a ring (Photos 2 and 3).

Ch 1. Sc x 24 into the ring (so over the chain stitches). You will have to scoot the stitches up a bit after every 8 or so, otherwise you won't fit 24 st's in (Photo 4 is before "scooting", Photo 5 is after "scooting", Photo 6 shows that all the stitches will fit!). Join to the first st with a sl st .

Sl st in each st around(Photo 7). If you are just planning on making a ring (for whatever reason), you will bind off at this point (Photo 8) and

Crochet Wreath Patterns

work away your tails of yarn. If you are making a teeny tiny wreath, however, don't bind off just yet.

The resulting ring will have a pretty braid running all the way around it. Because of the slip stitches, the edge will be nice and thick. The photo below (far right) shows what it will look like from the back.

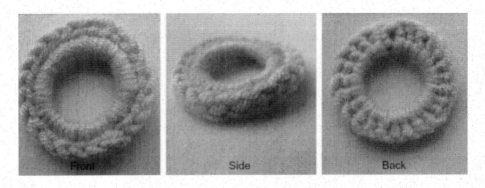

To turn your simple crochet ring into a tiny hangable wreath, you will need to ch 10 before binding off. THEN you can bind off, leaving a

Crochet Wreath Patterns

15 cm (6") tail of yarn. Use the tail of yarn to sew the end of the chain to the back of the wreath (right behind the stitch where the chain starts.

Now embellish your tiny wreath with embroidery or beads or glitter glue…whatever makes your creative heart happy.

Cream Merry Christmas Wreath

Materials

Lily Sugar'n Cream Cotton 4 ply Solids 2.5 oz [70.9 g]/Sparkles 2 oz [56.7 g]

Color A - (Red) 1 ball

Crochet Wreath Patterns

Color B - (Baby Pink) 1 ball

Color C - (White) 1 ball

Color D - (Mistletoe Sparkle) 1 ball

Small amount of blue yarn.

Note: 1 ball each of A, B and C makes 15 Santas.

1 ball each of A and C makes 7 Stockings.

1 ball of Sparkle makes 5 Gift Boxes.

Size 4 mm (U.S. G or 6) crochet hook or size needed to obtain gauge. Stuffing. Glue gun and glue sticks. 2 yds [1.8 m] of ⅝ inch [15 mm] wide green ribbon. 3 yds [2.75 m] of ¼ inch [10 mm] wide white ribbon. 20 small dried pine cones. Styrofoam Wreath 12 ins [30.5 cm] in diameter. 1 ball Sugar'n Cream (Emerald) to wrap Wreath (optional).

GAUGE

16 sc and 16 rows = 4 ins [10 cm].

Crochet Wreath Patterns

INSTRUCTIONS

SANTA (make 3)

Face: With B, ch 6. Join with sl st to form ring.

1st rnd: Ch 3. 7 dc in ring. Break B and join C in last dc. With C, 8 dc in same ring. Sl st in first dc.

2nd rnd: Ch 3. Sl st in top of first B st. *Ch 3. Sl st in top of next st.* Rep from * to * for all B sts. **Ch 5. Sl st into next C st.** Rep from ** to ** to complete ring. Fasten off.

Hat: With A, ch 9.

1st row: 1 sc in 2nd ch from hook. 1 sc in each sc to end of ch. 8 sc. Turn.

2nd row: Ch 1. Miss first sc. 1 sc in each sc to end of row. Turn.

Rep 2nd row until one st remains.

Fasten off.

Pompom: Join C with sl st to point of Hat.

Ch 4. Join with sl st to form ring.

1st rnd: Ch 1. 12 sc in ring.

Break yarn leaving 6 ins [15 cm] end. Thread yarn through a needle and draw through top of each st in ring. Draw up firmly and fasten off.

FINISHING: Sew Hat to Face as illustrated. Embroider two eyes using blue yarn.

STOCKING (make 4)

Cuff: With C, ch 13.

1st row: (RS). 1 sc in 2nd ch from hook. 1 sc in each ch to end of ch. 12 sc. Ch 1. Turn.

2nd row: 1 sc in each sc to end of row. Ch 1. Turn.

Rep 2nd row once more, joining A at end of last row.

Crochet Wreath Patterns

Leg: With A, 1 sc in each sc to end of row. Ch 1. Turn.

Rep last row until work from beg measures 3 ins [7.5 cm] ending with RS facing and omitting turning ch at end of last row. Fasten off.

Heel: With RS of work facing, miss first 9 sc. Join C with sl st in next sc. Ch 1. 1 sc in same sc. 1 sc in each of last 2 sc. Bring other side of leg around. Work 1 sc in each of first 3 sc. Ch 1. Turn.

Next row: 1 sc in each of first 4 sc. Ch 1. Turn.

Next row: 1 sc in each of first 2 sc. Ch 1. Turn.

Next row: 1 sc in each of next 2 sc. 1 sc in next sc of long row below. 3 sts. Ch 1. Turn.

Next row: 1 sc in each of next 3 sc. 1 sc in next sc of long row below. 4 sts. Ch 1. Turn.

Cont as for last 2 rows until 6 sts of Heel have been worked, omitting turning ch at end of last row. Fasten off.

Foot: With RS of work facing, miss first 3 sc of Heel. Join A with sl st in next sc. Ch 1. 1 sc in same sc. 1 sc in each of next 2 sc of Heel. Miss next sc of Leg. 1 sc in each of next 4 sc. Miss next sc of Leg. 1 sc in each of next 3 sc of Heel. Ch 1. Turn. 10 sts.

Next row: 1 sc in each sc to end of row. Ch 1. Turn.

Next row: 1 sc in each sc to end of row, changing to C in last sc. Ch 1. Turn.

Toe: Next 2 rows: With C, 1 sc in each sc to end of row. Ch 1. Turn.

Next row: (Draw up a loop in each of next 2 sc. Yoh and draw a loop through all loops on hook - Sc2tog made) 5 times. Fasten off.

FINISHING: Sew Cuff and Leg back seams. Sew Foot and Toe seams. Sew corners of Heel closed. Stuff lightly.

GIFT BOX (make 5)

Crochet Wreath Patterns

Box Main Piece: With D, ch 8.

1st row: 1 sc in 2nd ch from hook. 1 sc in each ch to end of ch. Turn. 7 sc.

**2nd to 6th rows: Ch 1. 1 sc in each sc to end of row. Turn.

7th row: Ch 1. 1 sc in back loop only of each sc to end of row. Turn.

8th to 10th rows: Ch 1. 1 sc in each sc to end of row. Turn.** 11th row: Rep 7th row.

Rep from ** to ** once. Fasten off.

Box Sides: (make 2)

Ch 7.

1st row: 1 sc in 2nd ch from hook. 1 sc in each ch to end of row. Turn. 6 sc.

2nd to 4th rows: Ch 1. 1 sc in each sc to end of row. Turn.

Fasten off.

FINISHING: Sew first row of Main Piece to last row to form a box with sides open. Sew one Box Side in position. Stuff Box. Sew remaining Box Side in position.

Tie a length of ribbon around Box, tie a bow, and stitch in place.

ASSEMBLY

If desired, wrap yarn around Styrofoam Wreath to cover completely. Using photo as a guide, glue Santas, Stockings and Gift Boxes on Wreath as illustrated. Glue on pine cones and ribbon bo

Cream Happy Thanksgiving

Materials

Lily® Sugar'n Cream

(Solids: 70.9 g / 2.5 oz)

Contrast A (00004 Ecru) 1 ball

Crochet Wreath Patterns

Contrast B (00095 Red) 1 ball

Contrast C (01130 Warm Brown) 1 ball

Contrast D (01628 Hot Orange) 1 ball

Contrast E (00082 Jute) 1 ball

Contrast F (00084 Sage Green) 1 ball

Note: 1 ball each of A, B, C and D will make 2 Turkeys.

1 ball will make 14 Small or 10 Large Pumpkins.

1 ball will make 25 Leaves.

Size 4 mm (U.S. G or 6) crochet hook or size needed to obtain gauge. Stuffing. 2 glue-on eyes.

Straw wreath 12 ins [30.5 cm] in diameter. Hot glue gun and glue sticks. Dried wheat sheaves for decoration. 1 yd [.9 m] 1¼ ins [3 cm] wide ribbon for bow.

GAUGE

16 sc and 16 rows = 4 ins [10 cm].

INSTRUCTIONS

TURKEY

Tail: With C, ch 8. Join with sl st to form ring.

1st row: (WS). Ch 2. 8 hdc in ring, changing to A in last hdc. Turn. 8 sts.

2nd row: With A, ch 1. (1 sc in next hdc. 2 sc in next hdc) 4 times. Turn. 12 sts.

3rd row: Ch 1. 1 sc in back loop only of each sc to end of row, changing to C in last sc. Turn.

4th row: With C, ch 2. 2 hdc in each sc to end of row. Turn. 24 sts.

5th row: Ch 3 (counts as first dc). Miss first hdc. 1 dc in each hdc to end of row, changing to A in last dc. Turn.

6th row: With A, ch 1. 1 sc in each dc to end of row. Turn.

7th row: Ch 1. 1 sc in back loop only of each sc to end of row, changing to C in last sc. Turn.

8th row: With C, ch 3. 1 dc in first sc. (Ch 1. 1 dc in next sc) 23 times. Turn.

Crochet Wreath Patterns

9th row: Ch 3. (Miss ch-1. 1 dc in next dc. Ch 1) 23 times. 1 dc in top of turning ch, changing to A in last dc. Turn.

10th row: With A, ch 1. 1 sc in first ch-1 sp. [Miss 1 dc. (1 hdc. 1 dc. 1 hdc) in next ch-1 sp. Miss 1 dc.

1 sc in next ch-1 sp] 11 times. Miss next dc. (1 hdc. 1 dc. 1 hdc) in next ch-1 sp. Sl st in top of turning ch. Fasten off.

BODY: (make 2 pieces alike)

With C, ch 15.

1st row: 1 sc in 2nd ch from hook. 1 sc in each ch to end of ch. Turn. 14 sts.

2nd row: Ch 1. 1 sc in each sc to end of row. Turn.

3rd row: Ch 1. Draw up a loop in each of next 2 sc. Yoh and draw a loop through all loops on hook - Sc2tog made.

1 sc in each sc to last 2 sc. Sc2tog. Turn.

4th and 5th rows: Rep 3rd row, changing to B at end of 5th row. Turn. 8 sts at end of 5th row.

Crochet Wreath Patterns

6th row: With B, rep 3rd row, changing to A at end of row. Turn. 6 sts.

7th row: With A, ch 1. 2 sc in first sc. 1 sc in each sc to last sc. 2 sc in last sc. Turn. 8 sts.

8th row: Ch 1. 1 sc in each sc to end of row. Turn.

9th and 10th rows: Ch 1. Sc2tog. 1 sc in each sc to last 2 sc. Sc2tog. Turn. 4 sts after 10th row.

11th row: Ch 1. (Sc2tog) twice. Fasten off.

BEAK: With D, ch 5.

1st row: 1 sc in 2nd ch from hook. 1 sc in each ch to end of ch. Turn. 4 sts.

2nd row: Ch 1. (Sc2tog) twice. Turn. 2 sts.

3rd row: Ch 1. Sc2tog. Fasten off.

Wattle: With B, ch 7. Fasten off.

LEGS: (make 2)

With D, ch 3.

1st row: Sl st in 2nd ch from hook. Sl st in last ch.

(Ch 3. Sl st in 2nd ch from hook. Sl st in last ch) twice.

Next row: Ch 1. Draw up a loop at base of each toe. Yoh and draw through all 4 loops on hook. Ch 4.

Sl st in 2nd ch from hook. Sl st in each of last 2 ch.

Fasten off.

Finishing: Sew Beak to Body as shown in picture.

Sew Wattle to base of Beak. Sew the two Body pieces tog, leaving bottom open, and stuff lightly.

Sew bottom closed. Sew Legs to bottom of Body.

Attach eyes and sew Body to Tail.

PUMPKINS (make 2 each of small and large)

Small Pumpkin Body:

With D, ch 4. Join with sl st to form ring.

Crochet Wreath Patterns

1st rnd: Ch 1. 8 sc in ring. Sl st to first sc.

2nd rnd: Ch 1. 2 sc in each sc around. Sl st to first sc. 16 sc.

3rd and 4th rnds: Ch 1. 1 sc in each sc around.

Sl st to first sc.

5th rnd: Ch 1. (Sc2tog. 1 sc in each of next 2 sc) 4 times. Sl st in first st. 12 sc.

Stuff with small amount of stuffing.

6th rnd: Ch 1. (Sc2tog) 6 times. Sl st in first st. 6 sc.

7th rnd: Ch 1. (Sc2tog) 3 times. Fasten off (bottom of Pumpkin).

Large Pumpkin Body:

With D, ch 4. Join with sl st to form ring.

1st rnd: Ch 1. 8 sc in ring. Sl st to first sc.

2nd rnd: Ch 1. 2 sc in each sc around. Sl st in first sc. 16 sc.

3rd rnd: Ch 1. (1 sc in next sc. 2 sc in next sc) 8 times.

Sl st in first sc. 24 sc.

Crochet Wreath Patterns

4th and 5th rnds: Ch 1. 1 sc in each sc around.

Sl st in first sc.

6th rnd: Ch 1. (Sc2tog. 1 sc in each of next 2 sc) 6 times. Sl st in first st. 18 sc.

7th rnd: Ch 1. (Sc2tog. 1 sc in next sc) 6 times.

Sl st in first st. 12 sc.

Stuff with small amount of stuffing.

8th rnd: Ch 1. (Sc2tog) 6 times. Sl st in first st. 6 sc.

9th rnd: Ch 1. (Sc2tog) 3 times.

Fasten off (bottom of Pumpkin).

STEM: (make 1 for each Pumpkin)

With E, ch 3.

Sl st in 2nd ch from hook. Sl st in last ch. Fasten off.

FINISHING

With D, sew through center of Pumpkin 5 times,

each time bringing yarn around the body at evenly spaced intervals. Draw tightly and fasten securely.

Sew Stem in place to foundation ch at top of Pumpkin.

LEAVES (make 4)

With F, ch 12.

1st rnd: (RS). 1 sc in 2nd ch from hook. 1 sc in next ch. 1 hdc in next ch. 1 dc in each of next 4 ch. 1 hdc in next ch. 1 sc in each of next 2 ch. 3 sc in last ch.

Working into other side of ch, proceed as follows:

1 sc in each of next 2 ch. 1 hdc in next ch. 1 dc in each of next 4 ch. 1 hdc in next ch. 1 sc in next ch.

2 sc in next ch. Join with sl st to first sc. Fasten off.

ASSEMBLY

Using photo as a guide, glue Turkey to base of Wreath. Glue one large and one small Pumpkin to Wreath on either side of Turkey with 2 Leaves under

Crochet Wreath Patterns

the Pumpkins, as shown in picture. Add wheat sheaves and ribbon bow.

Cream Happy Easter Wreath

Materials

Lily® Sugar'n Cream® (Solids: 2.5 oz/70.9 g; 120 yds/109 m; Ombres: 2 oz/56.7 g;

95 yds/86 m))

Crochet Wreath Patterns

Contrast A, B, C, D, E and F (assorted Ombre shades) 1 ball each

Contrast G White (00001) 1 ball

Note: 1 ball of Ombre makes 11 eggs.

Size U.S. G/6 (4 mm) crochet hook or size needed to obtain gauge. 2 yds of

mint ribbon ¼" [10 mm] wide for Lace Edging. Stuffing for eggs. 1 yd [.9 m]

of white, yellow, blue and mint ribbons ¼" [10 mm] wide for Eggs and Wreath.

Willow Wreath 14" [35.5 cm] diameter. Glue.

ABBREVIATIONS:

Approx = Approximately

Ch = Chain(s)

Dc = Double crochet

Rep = Repeat

Rnd(s) = Round(s)

Crochet Wreath Patterns

Sc = Single crochet

Sl st = Slip stitch

Sp(s) = Space(s)

Yoh = Yarn over hook

MEASUREMENT

Approx 14" [35.5 cm] diameter.

GAUGE

16 sc and 16 rows = 4" [10 cm].

INSTRUCTIONS

Eggs (Make 5 A, make 4 E, make 3 each of B and G, make 2 F, make 1 each of D and C.)

Ch 2.

1st rnd: (RS). 6 sc in 2nd ch from hook.

Join with sl st in first sc.

Crochet Wreath Patterns

2nd rnd: Ch 1. 1 sc in same sc as last sl st. (2 sc in next sc. 1 sc in next sc) twice. 2 sc in next sc. Join with sl st in first sc. 9 sc.

3rd rnd: Ch 1. 1 sc in same sc as last sl st. (2 sc in next sc. 1 sc in next sc)

4 times. Join with sl st in first sc. 13 sc.

4th to 8th rnds: Ch 1. 1 sc in same sc as last sl st. 1 sc in each sc around. Join with sl st in first sc. Stuff eggs firmly.

9th rnd: Ch 1. 1 sc in same sc as last sl st.

(Draw up a loop in each of next 2 sc.

Yoh and draw a loop through all loops on hook - Sc2tog made. 1 sc in next sc) 4 times. Join with sl st in first sc. 9 sc.

10th rnd: Ch 1. 1 sc in same sc as last sl st.

(Sc2tog over next 2 sts. 1 sc in next st)

twice. Sc2tog over next 2 sts. Join with sl st in first sc. 6 sts.

11th rnd: Ch 1. (Sc2tog) 3 times. 3 sts.

Fasten off.

Lace Edging (to fit Wreath 14" [35.5 cm] in diameter)

Crochet Wreath Patterns

With G, ch 142.

1st row: 1 sc in 2nd ch from hook. 1 sc in each ch to end of ch. 141 sc. Turn.

2nd row: Ch 1. 1 sc in first sc. *Ch 1. Miss next sc. 1 sc in next sc. Rep from * to end of row. Turn.

3rd row: Ch 1. 1 sc in first sc. *1 sc in next ch-1 sp. 1 sc in next sc. Rep from * to end of row. Turn.

4th row: Ch 1. 1 sc in each of first 2 sc.

*Ch 1. Miss next sc. 1 sc in each of next 3 sc. Rep from * to last 3 sc. Ch 1. Miss next sc. 1 sc in each of next 2 sc. Turn.

5th row: Ch 1. 1 sc in first sc. *Miss next sc. [(1 dc. Ch 1) twice. 1 dc. Ch 3. sl st in top of dc - Picot made. (Ch 1. 1 dc) twice] all in next ch-1 sp. Miss next sc.

1 sl st in next sc. Rep from * to end of row. Fasten off.

Join Lace in round. Thread mint ribbon through eyelets of 2nd row.

Wrap white ribbon around colored eggs and colored ribbons around white eggs as illustrated. Using photo as a guide, glue Lace Edging to

Crochet Wreath Patterns

Wreath as illustrated. Glue eggs to Wreath as illustrated. Glue 3 hanging eggs to ribbons and place in position as illustrated. Cut rem colored ribbons in 6" [15 cm] lengths. Fold in half and glue in position randomly around Wreath as illustrated.

Manufactured by Amazon.ca
Acheson, AB

15360684R00033